Chess

From first moves to checkmate

Chess

From first moves to checkmate

Daniel King

KINGFISHER

KINGFISHER

Kingfisher Publications Plc
New Penderel House,
283–288 High Holborn,
London WC1V 7HZ
www.kingfisherpub.com

Author
Daniel King

Editors
Clive Wilson
Vicky Weber (new edition)

Deputy Art Director
Mike Buckley

Production Manager
Oonagh Phelan

DTP Co-ordinator
Nicky Studdart

Picture Research Manager
Jane Lambert

Indexer
Hilary Bird

First published by Kingfisher Publications Plc 2000
This new edition published in 2004
1 3 5 7 9 10 8 6 4 2

A CIP catalogue record for this book is available from
the British Library.

ISBN 0 7534 1002 8

1TR/0404/TEC/MAR(MAR)/128MA/F

Printed in China

CONTENTS

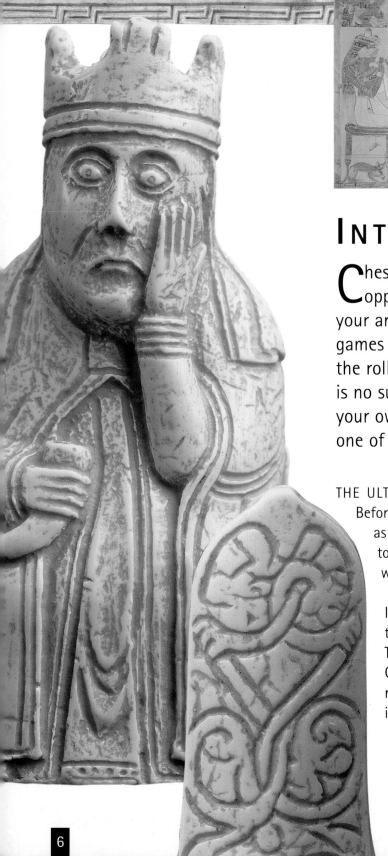

◁ *This Ancient Egyptian illustration shows that people have been playing board games for thousands of years.*

INTRODUCTION

Chess is a game of war. You control one army and your opponent, the enemy, controls the other. The fate of your army depends entirely on your own skill. Most other games rely on chance – a move may be determined by the roll of a die, or the turn of a card. But in chess there is no such thing as luck. You are entirely responsible for your own success or failure, and this is why chess can be one of the most satisfying of all games to win.

THE ULTIMATE GAME

Before you make a move on the chessboard you must try to predict as far as you can how your opponent will react. In deciding what to play, you will need to use reason, memory and logic combined with a dash of intuition and inspiration.

It has been calculated that there are more possible moves on the chessboard than the number of atoms in the universe. This helps account for the game's popularity through the ages. Chess has never been 'solved'. Even in today's computer age, it remains as complex and fascinating as it must have been when it emerged in India, almost fifteen hundred years ago.

From the 8th century until the 11th century, the Islamic world produced the best chess players. The Arabs were the first players to record their moves. Many of these games survive to this day.

'Chess is life in miniature. Chess is struggle, chess is battles.' Garry Kasparov World Chess Champion 1985–2000

THE ORIGINS OF CHESS

No one knows how the game of chess began. It is not clear whether it was invented by one person, or whether several different games gradually merged into one. Board games have been played for at least 6,000 years, but the game we recognise as chess can be traced back to India to around AD600. Its roots probably go back further. The game may even have emerged from a religious ceremony held in order to divine the balance between good and evil.

From northern India, chess spread quickly to Persia, and after the Arabian conquest during the 7th century, it reached the Arab world. Chess thrived in the Golden Age of Islam between the 8th and 11th centuries. The Arabs were great mathematicians, and the geometric nature of chess fitted in very naturally with their scientific interests.

Chess arrived in Europe by a variety of different trade routes, as well as the Moorish invasion of Spain in the 8th century and the Islamic conquest of Sicily not long after. The Vikings also took the game further westward. By the beginning of the 11th century, chess was already well-known across Europe.

The Isle of Lewis chess pieces date back to about the 12th century. They form the oldest surviving complete set. The pieces are carved from walrus ivory and depict characters in a variety of bad moods – from rage to gloom.

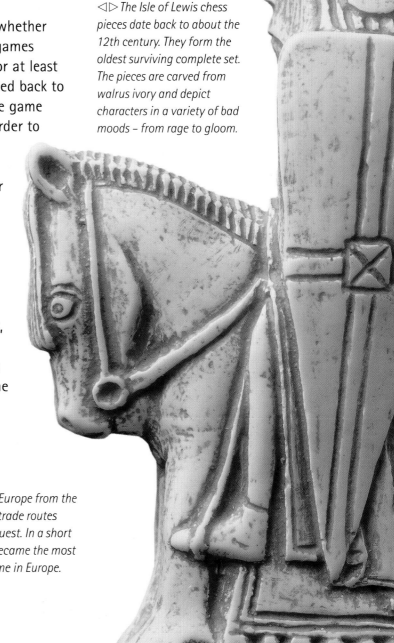

Chess came to Europe from the Arab world along trade routes and through conquest. In a short period of time it became the most popular board game in Europe.

THE EVOLVING GAME

During the later Middle Ages, between 1100 and 1450, chess established itself as the most popular board game in Europe – among the ruling classes. It was not until the 20th century that chess became a game played by millions of ordinary people.

△ *The earliest European study of chess is a Spanish work that dates from the late 13th century.*

▽ *When this Italian picture of two chess-playing sisters was painted in 1555, the rules of the game had settled into the ones we know today.*

A MIRROR OF SOCIETY

The names of the pieces that we use today – the king, queen, bishop and knight – were established during the Middle Ages when society was very ordered and geared towards warfare. Chess reflected this rigid world and it found a place in many ballads and poems of the period.

DYNAMIC CHANGES

After the 1450s, during the period known as the Renaissance, the rules of chess evolved into the ones with which we are familar. As society and cultural life became more dynamic, so did chess. The queen, which until then had had limited powers, now became the most powerful piece on the board. The bishop also extended its range and pawns were permitted to move two squares at the outset. These rule changes meant that a lightning attack was possible right from the very beginning of the game.

CHESS ON THE MOVE

Many different cultures and places have produced great chess players over the centuries. In the Renaissance, Spain and Italy were the strongest chess-playing nations. From the middle of the 18th century, Paris produced many excellent players and in the middle of the 19th century, when the British Empire was at its height, London became the centre of chess life. By the early 20th century, chess had ceased to be a game played exclusively by leisured and wealthy people. As chess became more democratic, centres of excellence sprang up all over the world – in central Europe (Berlin, Vienna, Budapest), in the Soviet Union and in North and South America. Chess had truly become a game for everyone.

LIVING HISTORY

In the long and varied history of chess, each generation has built upon the experience and knowledge of the preceding one. Records about the game have survived down the ages – they let us trace a clear line of thinking that goes right back to the earliest days of game. Whenever you play chess you are taking part in an ancient activity and making a direct link with players who lived almost 1,500 years ago.

Did you know ?

One of the first books printed in English by William Caxton was The Game and Playe of the Chesse, *in 1474.*

◁ During the long history of chess, the different pieces have inspired a wide variety of designs. These examples come from 18th-century Germany, 19th-century China and 20th-century Italy.

△ During the 19th century, chess clubs sprang up across Europe. Matches took place in coffee houses, important social meeting places at this time.

△ At the beginning of the 21st century, chess is played by millions of people across the world. The popularity of this age-old game continues to grow.

△ Computer chess has been a major innovation over the last two decades. Powerful chess-playing programs let you play against the machine and are a great way to improve your game.

SETTING UP

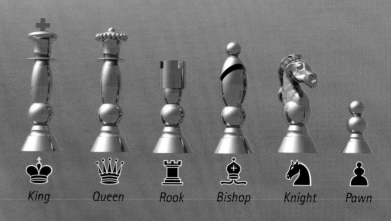

King   Queen   Rook   Bishop   Knight   Pawn

Chess is a game played by two players on a board of 64 squares, half of them white (or a pale colour) and the other half black (or dark). One player commands the white pieces, the other the black pieces, taking it in turns to move. White always makes the first move at the beginning of the game.

When positioning the board at the beginning of the game, make sure there is a white square in the right-hand corner. As well as being part of the rules, this helps you to set up the pieces for the start of the game.

The pieces are always set up in exactly the same way for the beginning of the game. On the first row of squares (or 'rank') stand the most important pieces. The rooks sit in the corners. Next to them on both sides of the board are the knights. Then come the bishops and finally, on the middle two squares, stand the king and queen.

Be sure to put the king and queen on the right squares. There is an easy rule to help you do this – the queen stands on its own colour. In other words, if you have a White queen it will be placed on the white square nearest the middle. If you have a Black queen it will stand on the black square nearest the middle. In front of these pieces, on the second rank, is a row of eight pawns.

Pieces should always be placed in the middle of the squares. Only one piece is allowed on a square at a time. However, enemy pieces can be captured by moving onto a square that is occupied and removing that piece.

◁ *In this book the chessboard and pieces are often represented by a simple diagram. If you are not sure which piece is which, you can refer back to the page opposite.*

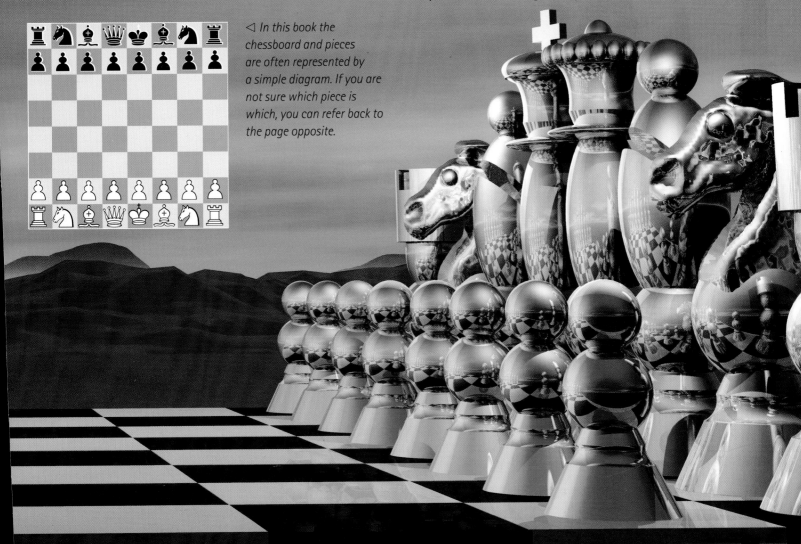

1

2

Test position

Which pieces can the White king take? Answer on page 60.

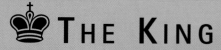 # THE KING

The king is easy to recognize. In most chess sets it is the tallest piece and it always has a small cross on the top of its crown.

The king is the most important piece on the chessboard. The whole game revolves around the struggle to trap the king into checkmate. Lose this piece and you lose the game, so it is vital that you keep the king as secure as possible. It is usually best to tuck the king away at the side of the board and surround it by a protective shield of pawns, just as political leaders in real life are protected by bodyguards. If a king loses the cover of its pieces, it is likely to fall prey to an attack by the enemy army because it cannot move out of danger very quickly.

The king is the most important piece, but it is actually one of the least powerful. It is only allowed to move one square at a time, although this can be in any direction. It can capture other pieces but it cannot move to a square where it can be captured, or be put in check itself. For now, just try to familiarize yourself with its basic moves (**diagrams 1 and 2**).

There is also one special move, or rather leap, that the king can make just once in the game. This is called castling and it is explained on page 26.

Did you know ?

Chess is sometimes known as the Royal Game – there is a legend that says the game was invented to amuse a king. Many kings and queens have played chess, including William the Conqueror, who is said to have broken a chessboard over a French prince's head.

♜ THE ROOK

At the start of the game you have two rooks in your army of pieces. They stand at the corners of the board looking like the turrets of a castle. Some players call the piece the 'castle', although the proper name is rook.

Rooks are powerful pieces, but at the beginning of the game they are unable to move at all because they are hemmed in by the other pieces. They really come into their own later on, when the game has opened out.

Rooks are able to move up and down, and side to side on the board unless there is something blocking their path. They cannot leap over other pieces, except when they perform the special move of 'castling' (see page 26).

In this position (**diagram 1**), the rook can move to any of the squares marked by the arrows. Compare the mobility of the rook to the limited range of the king. It is like the difference between a tortoise and a hare.

The rook can zoom from one side of the board to the other, but only if there is nothing in its way. Here, for instance, it cannot move past the White king (**diagram 2**).

1

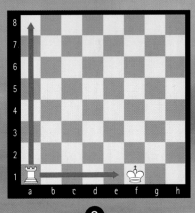

2

Did you know ?

The word 'rook' derives from an old Arabic word 'rukh', meaning chariot. By the time chess reached Europe, sometime after 700AD, chariots were no longer in use. Instead, the rook came to resemble a castle's turret, which more accurately reflected the nature of society and warfare during the Middle Ages.

Test position

Which pieces can the White rook take? Answer on page 60.

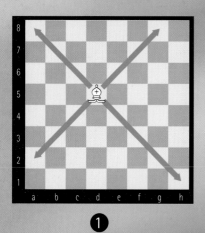

1

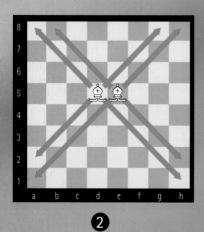

2

Test position

Which pieces can the White bishop take? Answers on page 60.

♝ THE BISHOP

Next to the king and queen at the start of the game you will find the bishops. This reflects their status in mediaeval society, when the clergy were at the heart of government, crucial advisors to the ruling monarchs.

The bishop may move forwards or backwards along the diagonals for as many squares as it likes, as long as there is nothing standing in its way. The bishop can move to any of the squares along the lines of the arrows (**diagram 1**).

Both sides have two bishops, one that runs along the dark squares of the board, the other on the light squares. A bishop that begins on a white square can only move along the white squares. A bishop that begins on a black square must keep to the black squares (**diagram 2**).

A 'bishop pair' can be very powerful in an open position, exerting influence right across the board. They are often best placed at the edges, far away from marauding enemy pieces, but still able to make their presence felt across the centre and the opposite side of the board.

Did you know ?

When the game of chess began in India, the bishops were known as 'elephants'. In many languages the name still survives to this day. In Russian, for example, the word 'slon', which means elephant, is used to refer to the bishop.

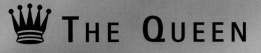

THE QUEEN

The queen is easy to recognize – it always has a crown at the top of the piece, and is just a bit shorter than the king, which it stands next to at the start of the game.

The queen is able to move up and down and across the board like a rook, as well as along the diagonals like a bishop, as long as there is nothing blocking its path. When it is in the centre of the board the queen exercises extraordinary power (**diagram 1**).

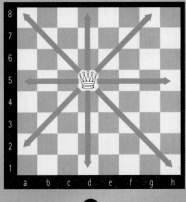

The queen does not have to stand in the middle of the board in order to have a decisive impact on the game. Even from the corner, the queen's influence stretches right across to the other side of the board. The queen is able to move to any of the squares along the marked arrows (**diagram 2**).

Although the king is the most important piece in your army, it is actually the queen that is the most powerful. This means that you should take good care of this piece – if the queen is lost, defeat is often inevitable. Try not to move the queen out too early in the game. First, make sure that you have found a safe square for it.

Did you know ?

In the original game in India and Persia, this piece – the 'vizier' – actually had very limited powers. However, after the 1400s, the queen became a more powerful piece, in keeping with a changing and more dynamic society.

Test position

Which pieces can the White queen take? Answers on page 60.

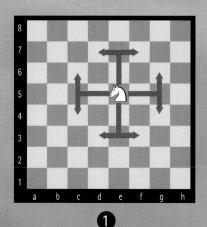

①

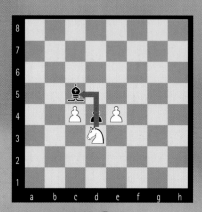

②

Test position

Which pieces can the Black knight take? Answers on page 60.

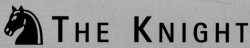

THE KNIGHT

The knight is one of the craftiest members of your army. It has the unique ability to leap over other pieces. This, combined with its side-stepping movement, can make it a difficult piece to deal with.

The knight moves two squares in a straight direction, and then one to the side, either to the left or the right. It might be easier if you think of the move as a kind of 'L-shape (**diagram 1**).

The knight makes the game more dynamic. In positions that appear blocked it can force a breakthrough because it is the only chess piece that is able to leap over other pieces. Here, for instance, it can capture the bishop that stands on the other side of the pawns (**diagram 2**).

Because the knight is a short-range piece, it often functions poorly at the side or the corner of the board, where its scope is limited. You will find that it is much more effective to keep your knights in the middle of the board where they have more options.

Did you know ?

As far as we know, the 'L-shaped' knight move has remained the same since the beginnings of the game in India at the end of the 6th century. This leaping piece has always been associated with the cavalry.

THE PAWN

Eight pawns stand in front of your pieces. They are the foot-soldiers, the least valuable members of your army. Nevertheless, they still perform a very important role in the game.

On their first move, pawns are able to advance either two squares, or one. After this, they are only allowed to move forward one square at a time (**diagram 1**). They cannot move backwards or sideways. Among other duties, pawns are used to mark out territory before the most important pieces advance into battle.

Unlike all the other pieces, pawns capture in a different way to how they normally move. They capture one square diagonally forward. Here, for instance, White could choose to take either the rook or the knight (**diagram 2**).

Pawns have one special property that can prove decisive in many games. If a pawn reaches the other side of the board, it must immediately transform into another piece – a knight, bishop, rook, or queen (**diagram 3**). In practice, most people choose a new queen as it is the most powerful piece on the board. Promoting a pawn occurs most frequently at the end of the game when there are fewer pieces to obstruct the progress of the pawn down the board.

Did you know ?

In the 1700s, the French player André Philidor called pawns 'the soul of chess'. He recognized that pawns, despite their limited mobility, can often determine the nature and outcome of a game.

1

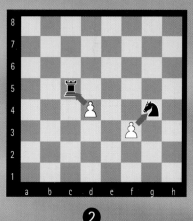

2

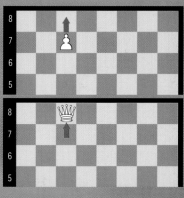

3

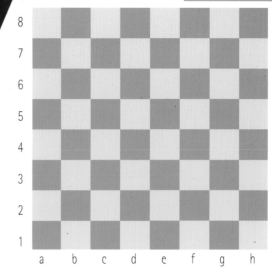

The rows of squares going up the board, the files, are each given a letter, from a to h. The rows of squares across the board are known as ranks. These are given a number from 1 to 8. Using this system, it is easy to identify each square on the chessboard with a letter and a number.

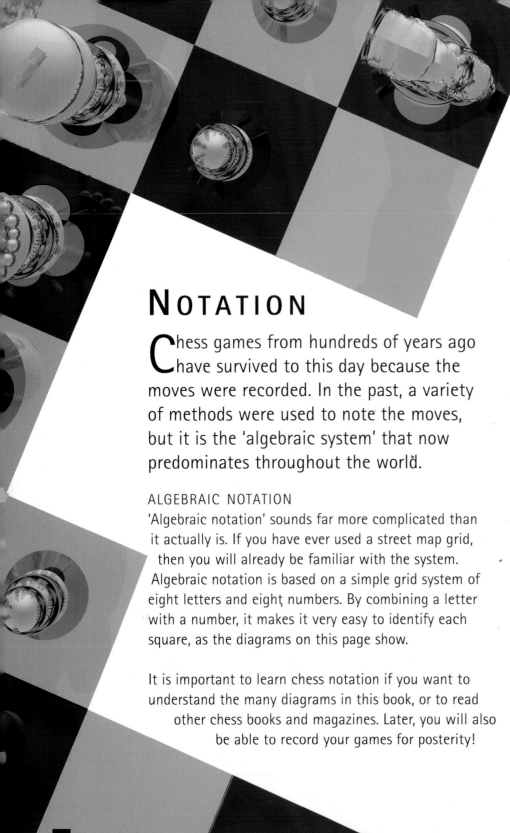

NOTATION

Chess games from hundreds of years ago have survived to this day because the moves were recorded. In the past, a variety of methods were used to note the moves, but it is the 'algebraic system' that now predominates throughout the world.

ALGEBRAIC NOTATION

'Algebraic notation' sounds far more complicated than it actually is. If you have ever used a street map grid, then you will already be familiar with the system. Algebraic notation is based on a simple grid system of eight letters and eight numbers. By combining a letter with a number, it makes it very easy to identify each square, as the diagrams on this page show.

It is important to learn chess notation if you want to understand the many diagrams in this book, or to read other chess books and magazines. Later, you will also be able to record your games for posterity!

For example, the square in the bottom right-hand corner is known as h1 – the letter is always put before the number. No matter which side of the board you sit at, the numbers and letters remain the same. The h1 square is always in White's bottom right-hand corner.

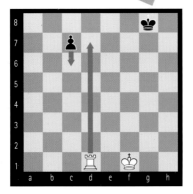

① *Take a look at this position. The rook moves up the board and Black responds by moving a pawn. These moves would be recorded in the following way:* **1 Rd7 c6**.

② *The **1** is the move number, the **R** stands for the rook, **d7** identifies the square the rook moves to. Black's move is given in the second column. The pawn moves to the **c6** square. Pawns are not identified by a letter – only the square they move to is recorded.*

Apart from the pawn, each piece is identified by a single capital letter:

K	King
Q	Queen
R	Rook
B	Bishop
N	Knight

*To avoid confusion with the king, the knight is given the phonetic **N**. The pieces are always identified with capital letters. For the squares, lower case letters are used.*

Here is a simple test. Set your pieces up for the start of the game and play out the following moves on your board (the x indicates a capture and the + means check).

1 e4 c5
2 Nf3 d6
3 d4 cxd4
4 Nxd4 Nf6
5 Bb5+ Nbd7
You should have reached the position in diagram 3.

③ *On the third move, notice that when Black's pawn captures, the file it comes from is noted (an exception to the rule that only the destination of the piece is recorded). In this case the pawn was on the c-file, and it captured a piece on the d4 square, so it is written* **3 ...cxd4**. *(The three dots are a standard convention to indicate that this is Black's move, not White's). On the fifth move, both of Black's knights could move to the d7 square, therefore a b is used to indicate which one goes there, in this case the knight standing on the b-file.*

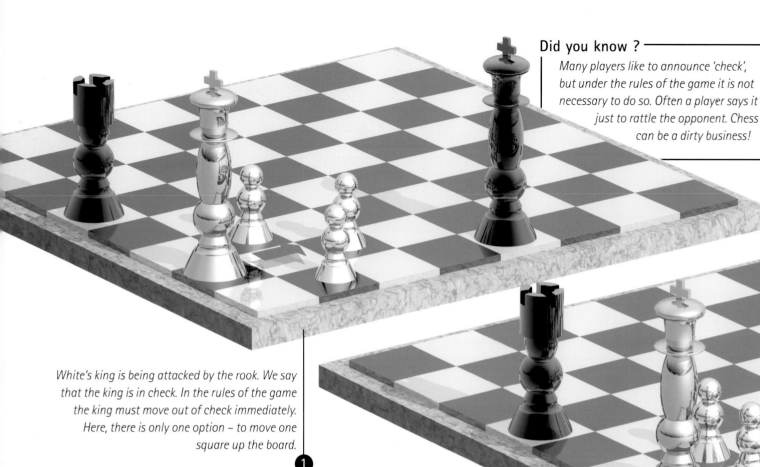

Did you know ?

Many players like to announce 'check', but under the rules of the game it is not necessary to do so. Often a player says it just to rattle the opponent. Chess can be a dirty business!

White's king is being attacked by the rook. We say that the king is in check. In the rules of the game the king must move out of check immediately. Here, there is only one option – to move one square up the board.

1

CHECK AND CHECKMATE I

Now that you know how the pieces move, it is time to tackle the principles of check and checkmate.

Checkmating your opponent's king is the ultimate aim in a chess game. The term derives from the ancient Persian 'shah mat' meaning 'the king is defeated'. You have to threaten the enemy king with one of your pieces so that it is unable to move and escape capture. Normally, a checkmate occurs when one side has an overwhelming superiority in forces, or through a direct and unexpected assault on the king.

This time, the position has changed a little. White's king is again in check from the rook, but now there is no escape. The king is trapped by its own pieces, it cannot move out of check, and so we say it is checkmated. The game is over and White has lost!

2

Checking is a little different. It occurs when the king is attacked by a piece, but can still escape. In other words, it is not necessarily fatal. The positions illustrated above demonstrate what the terms mean.

WHAT IS THE ADVANTAGE OF CHECKING?

Don't panic if your opponent suddenly thumps down a piece and cries 'check'. It does not end the game, and it is not always of benefit to your opponent. So what exactly is the point of checking?

- A check can help you gain time.
- Checking can drive the enemy king to a weak square, making it vulnerable to further attack.

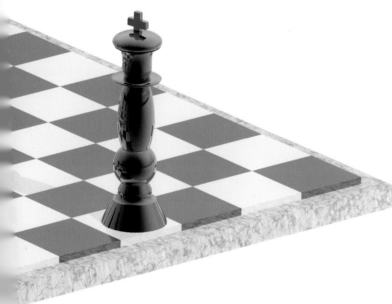

TEST POSITIONS

To make sure you understand the concepts of check and checkmate, here are six test positions for you to solve. You have to work out whether it is check or checkmate, and if it is only check, how do you escape? You will find the solutions on the following two pages, but before you turn to them have a go at solving the positions.

Did you know ?

If you fail to spot that you are in check, and do not prevent the attack to your king, it does not necessarily mean that you have lost the game. Your opponent has to let you take your move back. You must then play another move that gets you out of the check.

1 (Black to play)
Is this check or checkmate?

2 (Black to play)
Is this check or checkmate?

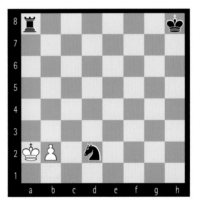

3 (White to play)
Is this check or checkmate?

4 (Black to play)
Is this check or checkmate?

5 (White to play)
Is this check or checkmate?

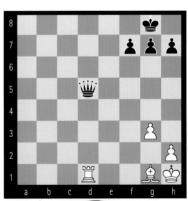

6 (White to play)
Is this check or checkmate?

21

1 *In this position, Black has been checkmated. White's knight is directly attacking the king, but the king is unable to escape because it is smothered by its own pieces.*

2 *Black has been checkmated here, too. The king is trapped in the corner and is in check from White's queen. It cannot take the queen, which is protected by the rook standing on g1.*

3 *White has been checkmated. The king is in check from the rook, and cannot escape. It cannot move to b3 or b1 – the knight has both squares covered.*

4 *Black's king is in check from the bishop, but it is not checkmate. The Black king can get out of danger by moving one square to the side.*

Check and Checkmate II
– Answers

The last three positions demonstrate the three methods of getting out of check – by moving the king, blocking the check, or capturing the piece that is checking.

When you are trying to figure out how to get out of check, remember these three key words – move, block and capture.

5 *White is in check but it is not checkmate. It is possible to advance the pawn on g2 one square to block the queen's check. Black would then be ill-advised to take the pawn on g3 with the queen – it is protected by the pawn on h2.*

6 *Black's queen is checking White's king in the corner of the board. However, it is not checkmate because White's rook can take Black's queen, leaving White with an overwhelming advantage.*

MATERIAL CHESS

Checkmating your opponent is the ultimate aim in a game of chess. But what is the best strategy to achieve this goal?

You will often find that your opponent's king is surrounded by a wall of pieces. When this happens a direct attack might not succeed. This is when a more effective strategy known as 'material chess' comes into play.

In most cases, for a checkmating attack to succeed, you need to have a superiority of forces. So, at first, your strategy should be to protect your own army. At the same time you should also be thinking of ways to trap and take your opponent's pieces. It is not advisable to go after the enemy king until you have a greater number of pieces than your opponent. So before each move, you need to ask yourself two important questions:

1) Can I capture any enemy pieces?

2) Are any of my pieces threatened?

Take a look at the following positions, keeping the above questions in mind.

3 *Imagine you are Black. Are any of your pieces under attack? Can you capture any of White's pieces?*

4 *None of Black's pieces are threatened so you are free to make an attack. There is a pawn on the b4 square which the bishop can snatch: 1 ...Bxb4. Black has won a pawn.*

5 *You might have noticed that Black can make another capture in diagram 3. The queen can take White's bishop on e3. Isn't it better to grab a bishop rather than a pawn?*

6 *Not in this case. White would then be able to capture the queen, winning a decisive advantage in pieces.*

1 *Imagine that you are White. Is Black threatening to take any of your pieces? Can you capture any of Black's?*

2 *There are no threats from Black, so White is free to send the queen to the other side of the board and capture Black's knight.*

The last example (**diagram 6**) leads us to an important aspect of chess – how much each piece is actually worth. The value of each piece is based on its power on the board. Remembering these values will help you decide which pieces to exchange, and which pieces to keep.

The queen, with its ability to move like a rook and a bishop, is by far the most powerful piece on the board. It therefore has the highest value: 9 points. Next comes the rook with 5 points. The bishop and the knight are both worth 3 points, and finally comes the lowly pawn, with just one point. Remember that these are just rough values. In some positions a bishop is far more effective than a knight - and vice versa. Even so, they provide a useful guide when we are trying to make a tricky decision in the heat of the battle.

For example, in the last diagram, it would make no sense to capture the bishop with the queen. White would gain a queen worth nine points, and only lose a bishop worth just three points. A good rate of exchange for White - but not for Black!

You will often win a game by first capturing more pieces than your opponent. You can then wear your enemy down to an endgame. At this stage of the game you are more likely to be in a position to promote a pawn into a new queen and only then launch an attack on the king.

But remember, chess games are not won just by gathering enemy pieces. Don't lose sight of the ultimate goal – checkmate!

VALUE

9 ——————————————————————————

5 ————————————————

3 ——————

3 ——————

1 ——————

SPECIAL MOVES

There is one special move during a game when both the king and the rook can leave their starting squares on the same turn. This move is called castling. It can be a highly effective way of protecting your king.

Castling brings the king, your most important piece, to a safe place at the side of the board. It also enables one of your most powerful pieces, the rook, to enter the game. All this with just one move!

You can castle on both sides of the board. Kingside castling (**diagrams 1 and 2**) is also known as 'short castling'. Queenside castling (**diagrams 3 and 4**) is called 'long castling' because there are more squares between the king and the rook on this side of the board.

1

The king moves two squares to the right along the first rank, and the rook leaps over and lands on the square next to it.

2

After castling, the king is at the side of the board. This is a much safer position than in the middle.

It is also possible to castle on the other side of the board. Once again, the king moves two squares along the first rank, this time to the left, and the rook leaps over and next to the king on the other side.

3

This is known as queenside castling or long castling. Notice that the king is not as deep in the corner as it is in kingside castling.

4

THE RULES OF CASTLING

Castling might appear a little tricky at first, but try to familiarize yourself with the rules as quickly as possible, as this is such a vital move.

- You cannot castle if your king has already moved.

- You cannot castle if your rook has already moved.

- You cannot castle if your king is in check on that turn.

- You cannot castle if your king lands into a check.

- Your king cannot castle through the line of another piece.

- You cannot castle if there is a piece standing in the way of the king or rook.

Here is an example of castling (**diagrams 5 and 6**) that should help make things clear.

Did you know ?

Even some of the greatest players have had trouble with the rules of castling! Viktor Korchnoi, for many years one of the strongest players in the world, once had to ask an arbiter if it was legal to castle. On another occasion, Korchnoi castled after he had already moved his king – definitely against the rules. His opponent also failed to notice that the move was illegal and the game carried on as if nothing had happened.

EN PASSANT

It's not only the rook and king that can make a special move. There is also an unusual kind of pawn capture, which is only available in a particular situation (**see diagrams 7 and 8**). The rule, which is known as 'en passant', is a legacy from five hundred years ago when pawns were first allowed to advance two squares on their opening move.

The 'en passant' capture is available only when a pawn advances two squares from its starting position on a file adjacent to an enemy pawn on the fifth rank.

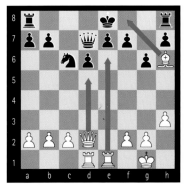

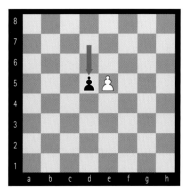

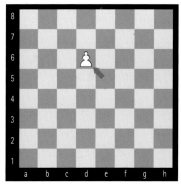

5 *Black's king is under severe pressure from White's rooks and queen in the middle of the board. It's time to evacuate the king from the centre. Black cannot castle on the kingside as the king is not allowed to move through the line of the bishop which covers the f8 square. However, it is possible to castle on the queenside.*

6 *A great side-step by Black's king. Castling has enabled the king to move closer to the security of the corner of the board, and Black's rook, which was languishing at the side, enters the fray.*

7 *If a pawn moves out two squares from its starting position, then an enemy pawn standing next to it on the fifth rank is able to capture it.*

8 *The White pawn moves one square diagonally behind the Black pawn, and removes it from the board. It's as if the Black pawn had only moved one square.*

If a player is to capture 'en passant', it must be done on the turn immediately after the opposition pawn has moved two squares or the option disappears.

OPENING THE GAME

Now that you have learned the basic principles of chess, you are ready to learn about the most effective ways of getting a game underway. This initial phase of the game is known as the opening.

At the beginning of the game most of your pieces are boxed in. Only the pawns, which stand in front of the other pieces, can move along with the knights, which are able to leap over the pawns to the third rank.

Here are the first few moves of a game where White does all the right things, and Black makes plenty of mistakes. But we can learn from those errors too!

1 **1 e4 e5** *Moving the pawn two squares to e4 is one of the best opening moves. The pawn not only controls crucial squares in the middle of the board, but it frees the way for the queen and bishop to enter the game. Black replies in the same way.* **2 d4.**

2 *A bold central advance by White, putting pressure on Black's centre and allowing the other bishop to enter the game.* **2 ...exd4   3 c3**

3 *Understandably, Black has captured the pawn in the middle of the board, and White replies by offering another! Was that wise?* **3 ...dxc3   4 Nxc3**

4 *Black grabs the second pawn and White recaptures with the knight. White is playing a 'gambit'. This is when a piece is given up in the opening in order to free up your other pieces.* **4 ...Nc6   5 Bc4   Nf6   6 Nf3**

5 White has brought out a bishop and a knight, and Black has brought out two knights. These are all strong moves as they help to control important squares in the centre of the board. **6 ...Qe7 7 0-0** *(This is how kingside castling is recorded.)*

6 Black's last move was dubious. The queen is in danger of being attacked by less valuable pieces, so for the moment it should not be moved. White's last move was excellent. Castling brings the king to the side of the board where it is protected by a row of pawns, and also brings the rook into play. **7 ...Nxe4**

7 Black falls for a trap! Another pawn is taken, but this opens the centre leaving the king in great danger. **8 Nxe4 Qxe4 9 Re1**

8 A total disaster for Black. The queen is attacked by the rook but is unable to move away as the king would then be in check. In other words, the queen will be lost. We say that the queen is 'pinned' to the king (there is more on the tactic of 'pinning' on pages 30–31).

White did well, but Black's play was poor. There are three opening principles that should be borne in mind when playing the first few moves of the game.

1) Control the centre

If you control the centre of the board, then you control the game. You will also find it easier to deal with any difficulties as the game develops.

2) Bring out your pieces

On the chessboard it is vital that your entire army comes into play as quickly as possible. If your pieces are too slow, the battle could be lost before you know it.

3) Get castled

Remember, your king is the most important piece but, at the same time, one of the least powerful. By castling as quickly as possible, it can be put in a safe position. You will also find that bringing the rook from the corner into play can be very useful in the fight for the centre.

DANGER!!

Do not move your queen out too early in the game. It is liable to be attacked and driven back by weaker pieces. Although the queen is your most powerful piece, it still needs the support of the rest of your army.

FORKS, PINS AND SKEWERS

Forks, pins and skewers are some of the sneakiest tricks you can use against your opponent. These tactics can lead to winning one, and sometimes several, enemy pieces. And, ultimately, this can lead to winning the game.

Although it is unlikely that you will find the positions on the opposite page duplicated exactly in your own games, you will soon begin to recognize similar positions. The more you play, the more familiar you will become with these highly effective and often deadly ruses.

THE FORK

This is a simultaneous attack on two enemy pieces. The most common fork is made by the knight (**diagram 1**). Knight forks feature in many games, so it is important to familiarize yourself with the move – for your own safety! Pawns can also make effective two-pronged attacks (**diagram 2**). The bishop and the knight are frequently the target of pawn forks.

THE PIN

The pin is an attack against two enemy pieces standing on the same line. Like the fork, this is also extremely common. We have already encountered a pin on page 29 (**diagram 8**). On that occasion, a rook pinned the queen to the king. This time (**diagrams 3 and 4**) the pin is a little different.

THE SKEWER

This can be a deadly manoeuvre. The skewer attack operates by piercing through one piece to trap another standing on the same rank, file or diagonal. The second piece is the real target (**diagrams 5 and 6**).

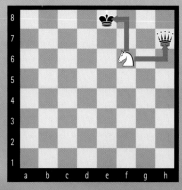

1 White's knight has leaped in, checking Black's king, and at the same time attacking the queen. Lethal! Black must move the king out of check, then the knight captures the queen on the next turn.

2 This is another example of a fork, this time by a pawn. Black's pawn has just advanced, simultaneously attacking the bishop and the knight. One of the pieces can be saved, but not both, so Black wins material. (Remember, a pawn is worth just one point and the bishop and knight three.)

3 Here is a very effective pin. Black's bishop has moved out to attack the queen. White's queen cannot escape as the king would then be in check. The best that White can do is to take the bishop with the queen – but then lose this key piece to the Black knight on the following move.

4 In this position, White's pawn moves up to attack the knight in a classic case of how to exploit a pin. If Black's knight moves, then the queen will be taken by the rook. There is no escape – the capture of Black's knight has become inevitable.

5 A skewer can be a deadly piece of play. Here, Black's king is in check from White's queen. The king must move out of check. White's queen will then capture Black's queen.

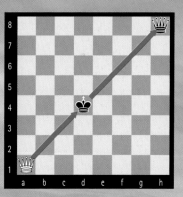

6 White's rook has just moved to b5, attacking the queen. The queen must move as it is Black's most valuable piece. But, when it does, White's rook can capture the exposed knight.

FOUR LETHAL ATTACKS

There are many cunning and devious ways to make an attack. Some occur with such frequency that they have been given specific names – as we have just seen. Here are a few more lethal weapons to add to your armoury.

DISCOVERED CHECK

Although it has a slightly confusing name (like a lot of chess jargon) this can be very effective. Discovered check is when one piece is moved . . . allowing another piece to give check (see diagrams 1 and 2).

1 *Look at the position of Black's rook in relation to White's king. It would be check if it weren't for Black's knight which sits in between the two. That gives Black an idea. The knight could be moved out of the way, putting White's king in check from the rook. Now comes the clever bit. Why not move the knight so that it attacks the queen?*

DIAGONAL BATTERY

You might think that a castled king position is quite safe. After all, it is at the side of the board, away from the exposed centre, and, in this case (**diagram 3**), protected by pawns. But a castled king is not invulnerable.

3 *White has craftily lined up a battery of fire-power – the queen is in front of the bishop on the so-called 'long diagonal'. In this position the White queen can inflict maximum damage.*

4 *Black's king cannot get out of check – the White queen is covered by the bishop. Checkmate! Here it was very easy for White to set up the battery of queen and bishop but, in the cut and thrust of battle, it may not be so simple. Even so, watch out for this deadly attack in your games.*

SEVENTH HEAVEN

At the start of a game, the rooks, trapped in the corners, struggle to make their mark on the game. However, later on, when pieces have been cleared from the board, the rooks play a more prominent role, zooming down open files. If they are able to reach the seventh rank, they can be extremely dangerous, capturing pawns and pinning the enemy king to the side of the board (diagrams 5 and 6).

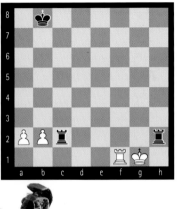

5 *The two Black rooks have both made it to the seventh rank. Nothing can stop them from sweeping up everything in their path. Now they even have the chance to deliver the final blow.*

6 *The rook sweeps over to deliver checkmate to the helpless king – it cannot capture the rook which is now supported by its comrade. Two rooks on the seventh rank are exceptionally powerful but even a single rook should not be underestimated.*

BACK RANK MATE

We now move one rank further down, from the seventh to the eighth, the last or 'back rank'. We already know that the sooner one castles in a game, the better. However, as we've seen, even after castling you must still take care.

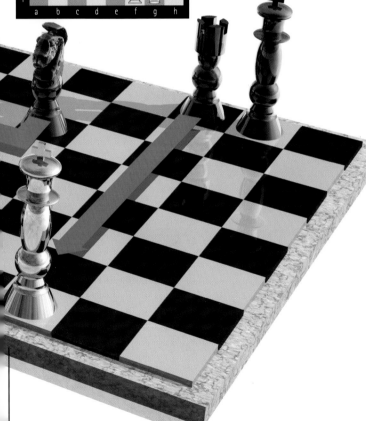

Brilliant! The knight has moved out of the way of the rook, putting White's king in check. The king must get out of check, then on the next turn Black's knight takes the queen, the most powerful piece on the board. This will leave Black with a rook and a knight against a lone king – more than enough pieces to force a checkmate.

7 *Black's rook has just moved to c8, threatening to capture the queen. At first glance, the move appears safe as the bishop covers the rook. But White has spotted that the back rank is vulnerable and sacrifices the queen:* **1 Qxc8+**. *Black must recapture with the bishop:* **1 ...Bxc8**. *Then the rook rockets to the eighth rank:* **2 Re8**.

8 *It's checkmate. Black's king is unable to escape from the rook's check – it is blocked in by its own pawns. Checkmate could have been avoided by pushing out one of the pawns in front of the castled king (as White has done in this position) so that the king has an escape route if there is ever a check on the eighth rank.*

SACRIFICE!

In chess, a sacrifice is when a piece is given up for greater gain. For instance, it might result in winning enemy pieces or, in the best case, even forcing a checkmate.

The word 'sacrifice' has associations with ancient religion – animals were once sacrificed on the altar to appease a god. You should keep in mind why a sacrifice is made – for the greater good of the community, in this case, your army of chess pieces, and the ultimate goal of checkmate. A sacrifice can come as a great surprise to your opponent. Just as in a real battle, surprise is one of the most useful weapons at your disposal.

Making a sacrifice is thrilling but it is also risky. For instance, you might miscalculate, so that when the smoke clears, the balance is negative – you are left with fewer pieces than your opponent. It is important, therefore, to weigh up the options carefully before committing yourself.

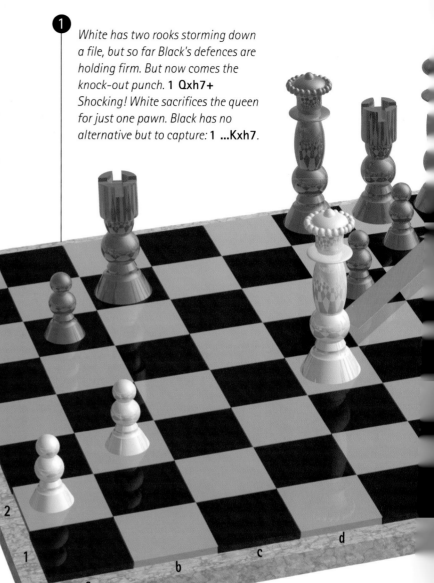

1 White has two rooks storming down a file, but so far Black's defences are holding firm. But now comes the knock-out punch. **1 Qxh7+** Shocking! White sacrifices the queen for just one pawn. Black has no alternative but to capture: **1 ...Kxh7**.

Did you know ?

In the history of chess, arguably the greatest exponent of the sacrifice was the Latvian, Mikhail Tal (1936–1992). He was able to conjure up an attack from nowhere by playing the most unexpected sacrifices. Here Tal (White) throws a knight into the middle of the board, inviting his opponent to capture it with the pawn. He realized that in return for the piece, the full force of the bishops would be unleashed on Black's king. In the end, Tal's opponent was unable to resist the pressure of the attack and lost the game.

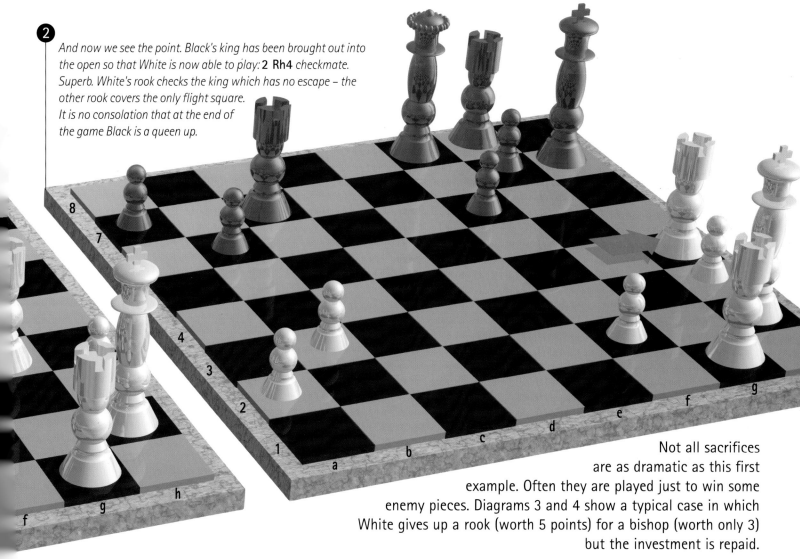

2 *And now we see the point. Black's king has been brought out into the open so that White is now able to play: **2 Rh4** checkmate. Superb. White's rook checks the king which has no escape – the other rook covers the only flight square. It is no consolation that at the end of the game Black is a queen up.*

Not all sacrifices are as dramatic as this first example. Often they are played just to win some enemy pieces. Diagrams 3 and 4 show a typical case in which White gives up a rook (worth 5 points) for a bishop (worth only 3) but the investment is repaid.

3 *White, with two extra pawns, is already doing well, but the easiest way to finish the game is to play **1 Rxf8+**. Black's king then takes the rook **1 ...Kxf8**. The point of the sacrifice is to set up a knight fork – Black's king has been forced to the perfect square: **2 Nd7+**. Black's king must now move out of check.*

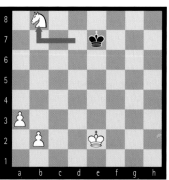

4 *2 ...Ke7 3 Nxb8. The knight captures the rook on b8, leaving White in a winning position. One of the pawns can eventually be forced to the eighth rank, making a new queen.*

Let's check the balance at the end of this skirmish. White gave up a rook (worth 5 points) but gained a rook and bishop (worth 5 and 3 points). White came out on top.

WHAT IS A DRAW?

When you play a game of chess, winning and losing are not the only possible outcomes. If neither side is able to force a checkmate, then the game is drawn. In serious tournament play, about half of all games end this way.

Just because a game is drawn it does not mean that it has not been hard-fought – it is inevitable that sometimes an Immovable Force meets an Irresistible Object! There are a number of ways in which a game may end in a draw.

INSUFFICIENT MATING MATERIAL
If neither side has enough pieces left at the end of the game, then the position is declared drawn (see diagram1).

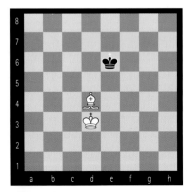

1 *For instance, here, the game is drawn as it is impossible to checkmate with just a lone bishop - you can try if you like, but you won't get anywhere! Likewise, king and knight against a king is a draw.*

As a pawn is less powerful than a knight, you might assume that king and pawn against king is also a draw – but this is not always the case. Sometimes it is possible to force the pawn to the eighth rank to get a new queen, and it is possible to checkmate with a king and queen. It is also possible to checkmate with a king and rook.

REPETITION OF POSITION
If the same position occurs three times in a game, then the player whose move it is can claim a draw (diagrams 2 and 3).

Black, with three extra pawns, is hoping for a win. However, White can force a draw. Black's king is in check from the queen, so must move. The king moves back one square: 1 ...Kg8. White continues pursuing the king: 2 Qd8+.

2

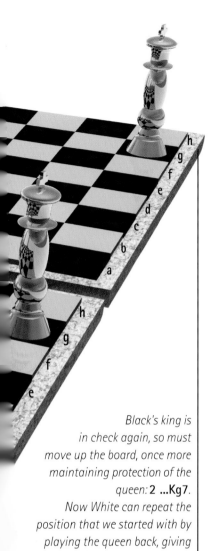

Black's king is in check again, so must move up the board, once more maintaining protection of the queen: **2 ...Kg7**. *Now White can repeat the position that we started with by playing the queen back, giving another check:* **3 Qd4+**. *This is the second repetition of the position. White repeats again:* **3 ...Kg8 4 Qd8+ Kg7**. *Now, White can claim a draw because the position can be repeated for a third time with the following move:* **5 Qd4+**. *A lucky escape.*

3

STALEMATE

Stalemate is something to watch out for when one side has an overwhelming superiority in forces, and is moving in for a checkmate against an exposed king. Stalemate is when a player cannot make any legal moves but is not in check (**diagrams 4, 5 and 6**).

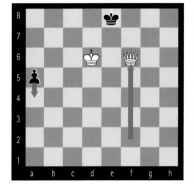

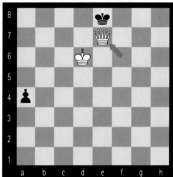

4 *With an extra queen against a lone king, White is hoping for a swift checkmate. White closes in with the queen for the kill, but comes a bit too close. Black's king has no legal moves. However, this does not mean that Black is checkmated. The king is not in check - this is the crucial difference. This position is 'stalemate' and is a draw.*

5 *This is the same position as the last one, with the crucial difference that Black has one remaining pawn. Again, White's queen closes in, and this time it is strong. Although Black's king cannot move, the position is NOT stalemate. Black still has one legal move:* **1 ...a4**, *then White's queen delivers checkmate:* **2 Qe7**.

6 *As you can see from this position, a single pawn can make all the difference between winning and drawing.*

THE FIFTY-MOVE RULE

This is an extremely rare way of making a draw. If a piece is not captured and a pawn is not moved for 50 moves then the game may be declared drawn. This is a very rare occurrence – games of chess are not usually so boring!

AGREEING ON A DRAW

The most common way to make a draw in serious tournament games is simply by agreement. After making a move, a player announces: 'I offer a draw'. This can either be accepted or declined. However, all too often, draws are offered and accepted as a way of playing it safe. It is better not to get into the habit of offering draws – cutting the game short unnaturally does nothing for your chess development.

TRAINING EXERCISES

In every serious sport you need to train regularly if you want to improve your game. Chess is no exception. Just like boxers training for an important fight, the strongest chess players in the world will spend months in preparation for a World Championship final, studying their opponent's style and strategy, and working on their own game.

WORKING OUT

There are simple exercises you can practise that will be of enormous benefit. You can either find a friend to play against or, if you have a chess computer, input the positions and use the machine as your sparring partner.

It is extremely important to learn how to finish off your opponent at the end of the game – the techniques explained here will help you feel confident about winning.

Even when you are practising these training exercises, try not to take any of your moves back. The following three-step plan will help you sharpen your chess mind.

1) Eyes   2) Brain   3) Hand

1) Look at the position carefully, paying particular attention to your opponent's last move.

2) Then work out what you think is the correct move.

3) Only when you are absolutely sure of your move should you reach for a piece.

First of all, have a go at checkmating with a queen and rook against a lone king (**diagram 1**). After you have tried this, take a look at the method explained below.

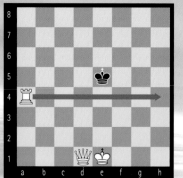

1 **1 Ra4.** *An important first move. Instead of checking, the rook restricts the king, preventing it from moving into one half of the board. Only then it will be driven back by the queen.* **1 ...Kf5 2 Qd5+ Kf6 3 Ra6+ Ke7 4 Qb7+ Ke8 5 Ra8** *You should have arrived at the following position (**diagram 2**).*

2 *Black's king is in check from the rook. It is unable to escape as the queen covers all the squares on the seventh rank. Therefore, the position is checkmate. If you have practised this mate and feel you have mastered it, try the same thing but with two rooks against a king. Use the same technique but you need to be a little more careful.*

Your next exercise is a little harder than the first. You have to force checkmate using your king and queen against a lone king. It is White to play.

TIP: It is impossible for a queen to deliver checkmate on its own. It needs the assistance of the king.

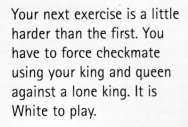

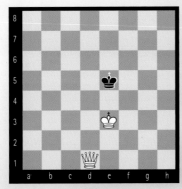

3 *1 Qd4+. It is only possible to checkmate the king at the side of the board, so first it must be driven there. The queen gives a check, forcing the king backwards.* **1 ...Ke6 2 Kf4 Kf7 3 Qd6**

4 *Instead of checking the Black king (which in this case would only allow it to escape up the board), the queen restricts its movement. Black's king cannot escape across the force-field created by White's queen.* **3 ...Kg7 4 Kf5**. *With Black's king trapped it is time to bring up the henchman to assist in the finish.* **4 ...Kf7 5 Qd7+ Kf8 6 Kg6 Kg8 7 Qg7**

5 *Black's king is in check from the queen, and there are no escape squares. The queen cannot be captured as White's king supports it. (Remember that the kings cannot stand on adjacent squares.) Therefore it's checkmate. The final position clearly shows how the attacking side must use the king to force checkmate.*

When there are just a few pieces on the board, the king becomes a powerful piece – in stark contrast to its role early on in the game when it should be hidden away as quickly as possible. The next training exercise aims to develop your skill in handling the king.

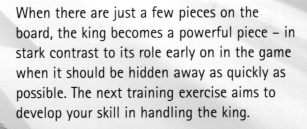

6 *Both sides have just a king and four pawns each. Your play needs to be subtle and highly skilled if you are going to win. You need to capture an enemy pawn with the king, then force one of your own pawns to the eighth rank to get a new queen. Then you can force a checkmate - using the techniques above.*

If you feel like increasing the complexity of the position, add a few more pawns to each side. This exercise is a great way of learning how the king and pawns interact.

TEST POSITIONS

To find out how much you have learned from the first half of the book, try solving these ten test positions. You will find some easy, but others require a little bit more concentration. Try to work out the answers in your head by just studying the diagrams on these pages. If you have problems visualizing the line of play, you can always set up the positions on your chessboard. Solving chess puzzles like these is an excellent way of sharpening your skills. You will find the answers on page 60-61.

1 Of all the possible pawn moves Black could make in this position, which is the best?

2 Black can make many different captures in this position. Which one is the best?

3 White is ready to launch a violent assault with moves such as **Re1+** or **Qxd6**. How can Black best counter White's threat?

4 White's rook is in a great position on the seventh rank. How can this be used to gain a winning material advantage?

5 It's White's turn to play. How does White get a winning advantage from this position?

6 What should Black play here?

7 White, to play, can gain a winning advantage with the next move. Can you see how?

8 Black has just moved a pawn forward, attacking White's knight. How would you respond?

9 How does White gain a winning material advantage from this position?

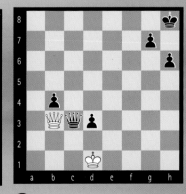

10 White is four pawns down – can the situation still be saved?

▷ *The World Chess Champions and the years in which they held the title.*

Wilhelm Steinitz
1886–1894

Emanuel Lasker
1894–1921

José-Raoul Capablanca
1921–1927

Alexander Alekhine
1927–1935,
1937–1946

Max Euwe
1935–1937

Mikhail Botvinnik
1948–1957,
1958–1960,
1961–1963

THE WORLD CHAMPIONSHIP I

Every great chess player dreams of becoming the World Chess Champion. The winner of the fiercely fought World Championship joins an illustrious list of previous title holders that goes back over a century.

CONTESTED BEGINNINGS

In 1866, a self-confident Austrian called Wilhelm Steinitz beat the German player Adolf Anderssen in a challenge match in London and duly proclaimed himself 'World Chess Champion'. There had never been an official World Champion before, and it was far from clear whether Steinitz should be the first. Then in 1883, Johannes Zukertort, a German who had won a few tournaments in Europe, pulled a similar trick, and also claimed to be 'World Champion'. Steinitz took offence, and a match was arranged in the USA, in 1886, with the title going to the first player to win ten games. The offical World Championship was born.

THE HIGHEST HONOUR

Steinitz won the match, and since then there has been a clear line of successors to the title. World Champions are accorded a huge amount of respect in the chess world. There can be gaps of many years between World Championship matches, so when they take place they generate a great deal of excitement. The matches can take weeks and sometimes months to complete.

Vassily Smyslov
1957–1958

Mikhail Tal
1960–1961

Tigran Petrosian
1963–1969

Boris Spassky
1969–1972

Bobby Fischer
1972–1975

Anatoly Karpov
1975–1985

Garry Kasparov
1985–2000

Wilhelm Steinitz (1836–1900) introduced a new positional style to the game. This Austrian player realized it was not necessary to go for an all-out attack on the king in order to win.

Emanuel Lasker (1868–1941) held the title for a record 27 years. Born in Germany, he was a great psychologist at the chess board, playing the man not the board. His greatest strength lay in the middle game.

José-Raoul Capablanca (1888–1942) combined his chess-playing life with that of a diplomat for his native Cuba. He favoured clear, simple positions and there was an effortless quality to his victories.

Alexander Alekhine (1892–1946) fled the Soviet Union in 1921 and later settled in Paris. Alekhine was obsessed by the game and studied chess eight hours a day. His style of play was explosive and dynamic. He died penniless in 1946, although still in possession of his title.

Max Euwe (1901–1981) was a mathematician from the Netherlands who won his first tournament when he was ten. An extremely logical player he held the title for only two years.

Mikhail Botvinnik (1911–1995) has been called the 'Patriarch of Soviet Chess'. He was a scientist by training and his study of all phases of the game, including the opening, was always painstaking.

Vassily Smyslov (1921–) was born in Moscow. He was a highly effective player of the endgame. In many ways he was the natural successor to Capablanca.

Mikhail Tal (1936–1992) became World Champion at the age of 23 with a style of chess that was flashy and fearless. His clashes with fellow Soviet player Botvinnik proved highly memorable.

Tigran Petrosian (1929–1984) was born in Armenia, in the former Soviet Union. His style of play was defensive and he was extremely hard to beat.

Boris Spassky (1937–) was born in Russia. He had an effortless, natural style, but he could never match the dedication of his great rival, Bobby Fischer.

Bobby Fischer (1943–) became the youngest winner ever of the US national championship at the age of 14. After he won the World Championship he dropped out of competitive chess and became a virtual recluse.

Anatoly Karpov (1951–) learned to play chess when he was four and studied with Botvinnik in Moscow. He is a great natural player, more at home defending than attacking.

Garry Kasparov (1963–) was born in Azerbaijan, in the former Soviet Union, and became the youngest World Champion ever at the age of 22. His chess is extremely dynamic and powerful.

Vladimir Kramnik (1973–) is a former pupil of Kasparov. Known as 'Iceberg' for his coolness under pressure, he makes his pieces work together in perfect harmony.

THE WORLD CHAMPIONSHIP II

When a World Championship match is played, millions of chess enthusiasts follow the games. Knowing that so many people are watching can inspire the players to perform brilliantly – or to collapse completely.

Petrosian (White) gives away his queen: 30 Qh8+. A neat temporary sacrifice to drag Black's king onto a poor square. Spassky resigns immediately: after 30 ...Kxh8 31 Nxf7+ a deadly knight fork occurs. Black's king must get out of check: 31 ...Kg7 but then the knight takes the queen: 32 Nxg5.

THE BEST MOVE IN A WORLD CHAMPIONSHIP?
The standard of play in World Championship matches has been, as one would expect, incredibly high, so it is difficult to select one move above thousands. However, this is one particulary memorable move (**diagram 1**). It is from the 1966 match between Tigran Petrosian and Boris Spassky. Petrosian finishes off his opponent in style.

1

2 *This leaves White with an extra knight and a pawn – at this level more than enough material advantage to force a win.*

THE WORST MOVE IN A WORLD CHAMPIONSHIP?
As well as many great moves there have also been a number of outright blunders. Under pressure, even the top players in the world can play some appalling moves. This miscalculation (**diagram 3**) is from the bitter World title fight in 1978 between Viktor Korchnoi, the challenger and Soviet defector, and his archenemy, Anatoly Karpov.

Although Karpov (Black) threatens a back-rank mate with his rook, this can be prevented quite easily by moving the g-pawn, providing an escape square for the king. Instead, Korchnoi blunders. He plays 39 Ra1, allowing a smart finish: 39 ...Nf3+, and Korchnoi resigns the game immediately. For if 40 gxf3, then 40 ...Rg6+ 41 Kh1 Nf2

3

WHO IS THE CURRENT WORLD CHAMPION?

In November 2000, Vladimir Kramnik, from Moscow in Russia, defeated Garry Kasparov in a sixteen-game match for the world title. As Kasparov had been rated number one in the world since 1985, Kramnik has a strong claim to be the legitimate World Champion. However, Kramnik has not defended his title since then.

On the other hand, there is Ruslan Ponomariov from the Ukraine who won the FIDE (Fédération Internationale des Échecs) world title in 2002. He came first in a huge knockout tournament in Moscow; however, neither Kramnik nor Kasparov participated. Ponomariov was only 18 years old at the time.

FIDE is the world governing body of chess. Since 1948, it has held regular contests for the world title. However, Kasparov broke away from FIDE in 1993 to organize his own world championship matches. Several attempts have been made to create a single world title by holding a champions' match. However, through a combination of battling egos, politics and a lack of sponsorship, nothing has taken place yet.

△ Mikhail Botvinnik and David Bronstein sit centre stage at the Tchaikovsky Concert Hall in Moscow, in 1951, battling it out for the ultimate title.

△ Karpov and Kasparov fought against each other five times in World Championship matches between 1984 and 1990, playing a total of 144 games.

White's king is trapped in the corner. Checkmate.
4

CONFUSED? YOU WILL BE . . .

So, is the World Champion Kramnik or Ponomariov? The answer is neither of them according to the House of Representatives of the USA. On March 13, 1986, it passed a resolution '. . . that the US government recognizes Bobby Fischer as the official World Chess Champion.'

Fischer won the World Title in 1972, but it was stripped from him in 1975 by FIDE when he refused to play against the challenger, Karpov. Nevertheless, he still claims to be World Champion, and the US government supported him, at least in the 1980s.

▷ Bobby Fischer, the brilliant US player, won the title in 1972 but since then he has hardly played.

Just to complicate matters, there are some people who think that a computer should be named World Chess Champion! On pages 56–57 you can read about *Deep Blue*, the computer that beat Kasparov.

THE GREATEST

In many sports there is often one personality who stands out as The Greatest. In boxing, most people would pick Muhammad Ali; in football it would be Pelé; and in chess you would have to choose Garry Kasparov. In 1985, at the age of 22, he became the youngest ever World Chess Champion by beating the reigning champion Anatoly Karpov. Kasparov successfully defended his title on five occasions. However, in 2000, he was finally defeated by his protégé Vladimir Kramnik.

△ Garry Kasparov salutes his cheering fans moments after winning the final decisive game of the 1985 World Championship match. He was awarded the winner's wreath (above) for the first time in his career.

EARLY YEARS

Kasparov was born in 1963 to a Russian Jewish father and Armenian mother in Baku, the capital of the former Soviet Republic, Azerbaijan. At the age of five he learned the moves of chess just by watching his father play. He progressed rapidly. At this time, the Soviet Union, with its strong chess tradition, was the best place in the world for a talented chess player to grow up. From an early age, Kasparov was able to receive top quality tuition. His rise to the top of the chess world was meteoric.

This was the final position from the 24th and final game of the 1985 match. Kasparov (Black) has just moved his knight away from the c2 square so that the rook checks Karpov's king – a classic case of a discovered check. At this point, Karpov resigned the game and with it the chess crown. When White's king moves, the knight will capture White's rook on e6 leaving Black in a winning position.

▽ At the age of 19, Kasparov already had a charismatic presence at the board, impressing his opponents with his enormous confidence and sheer will to win.

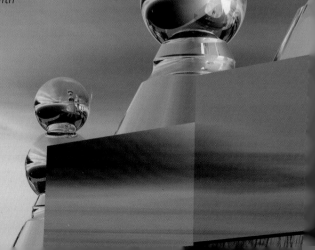

KASPAROV'S STYLE

When Garry Kasparov arrived on the international chess scene in the late 1970s and early 1980s, he was completely unstoppable. He did not just beat the opposition, he destroyed it. Most chess in the 1970s had been about grinding down one's opponent without taking risks. Kasparov's play was completely different – dynamic, explosive and fearless.

△ In the 1993 World Championship match, Kasparov faced a new challenger – the English player, Nigel Short.

CAREER RECORD

1963	Born in Baku, in the Soviet Republic of Azerbaijan.
1968	Learns the moves of chess.
1975	USSR Junior Champion.
1980	World Junior Champion; gains Grandmaster title.
1984	First challenges Karpov for the World title.
1985	Match abandoned in February after five months due to Karpov's exhaustion.
1985	Kasparov wins re-match six months later to become youngest World Champion ever at 22.
1986	Defeats Karpov in London and Leningrad
1987	. . . and again in Seville
1990	. . . and again in New York and Lyons.
1993	A new challenger – defeats Nigel Short.
1995	Defends title against Anand in New York.
1997	Defeated by *Deep Blue* in New York.
1999	Defeats leading rivals in four top tournaments.
2000	Loses world title to Kramnik in London.

THE SOVIET OUTSIDER

Chess and politics have always been closely bound up in the Soviet Union. For the Soviet authorities Kasparov was a concern. He was outspoken, too outspoken. In his first World Championship encounter with Anatoly Karpov in 1984, the Soviet Sports Committee intervened and halted the match when it looked as though Karpov - their loyal favourite - was crumbling through exhaustion. One Soviet bureaucrat said at the time, 'We have one World Champion, we don't need another', particularly if it was going to be one who chose not to follow the party line.

In 1990, Kasparov was forced to flee from his home in Baku on the Caspian Sea when Azeri nationalists took over the city. He chartered a plane from Moscow to bring out as many people as possible from the threatened Armenian community. Since then, he has lived with his family in Moscow.

Although he lost the world title in 2000, Kasparov has had more impact on the chess world than anyone before him.

THE SHORTEST AND LONGEST GAMES

A game of chess can be decided in just a few moves - or it might take hundreds. And the play can be as quick or as slow as the players wish. One of the most popular forms of chess is 'blitz' where both players have a total of five minutes to make all their moves. And for some players even that isn't fast enough . . .

THE SHORTEST GAMES

The quickest checkmate can be achieved in just two moves - but only with a hugely cooperative opponent, so don't raise your hopes. It is no wonder that this checkmate is called Fool's Mate (**diagram 1**).

1 1 g4 e5   2 f3 Qh4
checkmate. The king, boxed in by its own pieces, has no escape. Dreadful play from White! At the start of the game pawns should always be advanced from the centre of the board, not from the side.

A quick checkmate that is more useful to know about is Scholar's Mate. This attack is not recommended - it can rebound horribly - but you should be aware of it in case someone springs it on you (**diagrams 2, 3 and 4**).

2 1 e4 e5   2 Bc4
Sensible opening moves from both sides so far. The pawns advance in the middle and the bishop arrives at a good square. 2 ... Bc5   3 Qh5

3 *Black also plays the bishop out and White brings the queen into the game, threatening the pawn on e5 and checkmate on f7. If Black moves the queen to e7 both threats would be covered. But instead, Black makes a poor move:* 3 ...Nc6   4 Qxf7

4 *Checkmate. Black spotted that the e-pawn needed defending and covered it with the knight, but missed the bigger threat - checkmate on f7. The Black king cannot take the queen because it's supported by the bishop. A checkmate that could have been avoided.*

THE LONGEST GAME

Most modern tournament games now have an imposed time limit of seven hours. Previously there was no limit. In 1989, one game played in serious competition lasted 20 hours and 15 minutes and took 269 moves. And the result of this lengthy game? A draw.

THE MOSCOW MARATHON

The longest-ever World Championship final took place during 1984–1985 and involved the two Soviet players Anatoly Karpov and Garry Kasparov. The first to win six games would be declared the winner. However, after winning five games, Karpov was unable to finish off Kasparov. At one point, there were 17 draws in a row. Eventually, after 48 games, the match was abandoned with Karpov suffering from physical and mental exhaustion. In the return match, later in 1985, a maximum limit of 24 games was re-introduced, much to everyone's relief.

◁ The 1984–1985 World Championship final between Karpov (left) and Kasparov (right) lasted a gruelling five months. Even the Russian chess public lost patience at one point, booing and wolf-whistling the two players.

CORRESPONDENCE CHESS

One form of chess that breaks all longevity records is correspondence chess. Players post their moves to each other. Three days is generally allowed before responding. Some games take years to finish. It is not unknown for players to die before a game has been completed!

SPEED CHESS

At the other extreme, the first one-minute world championship ('bullet chess') was organized in 1999. The rules are simple – you have to play ALL your moves in one minute or you lose the game. (If you are interested, check out the Internet Chess Club on www.chessclub.com.)

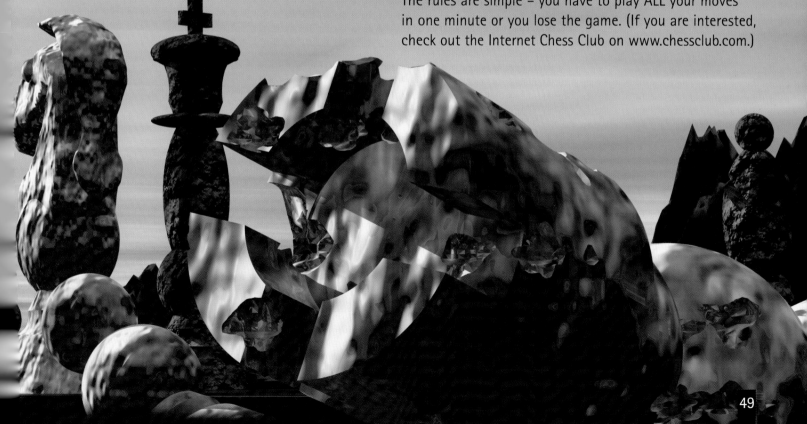

STARERS AND SHAKERS

Such are the passions aroused by chess that, occasionally, some players even break the rules in order to win. However, much more common than outright cheating is 'gamesmanship'. This is the art of unsettling your opponent, but staying within the rules of the game. As long ago as 1561, Ruy Lopez, one of the best players of his age, suggested positioning the board so that the sun shines in your opponent's eyes!

△ In 1977, the Soviet player Tigran Petrosian had a bruising encounter with the Soviet defector Viktor Korchnoi, involving table-shaking and the use of feet!

UNSPORTING BEHAVIOUR?

A fairly common tactic is for a player to develop certain exaggerated mannerisms at the board. You might recognize the following types.

The **piece-thumper** will smash a piece down right in the heart of your army, usually to distract your attention from elsewhere on the board.

The **face-puller** will cast a bemused look at your move, and follow with a quick reply and an amused smile.

The **starer** is more intimidating. World Champion Mikhail Tal's penetrating stare unnerved one opponent so much that he countered by wearing reflective sunglasses.

The **table-shaker** can be equally unsettling. It is difficult to concentrate properly when the pieces are wobbling! Tigran Petrosian used this tactic against Viktor Korchnoi in 1977. Korchnoi asked him to stop, but Petrosian responded by turning off his hearing aid. Korchnoi replied with a swift kick under the table. For the next game a partition was built under the table.

PUSHING THE LIMITS

The chess match that inspired the most gamesmanship was the 1978 World Championship final between Anatoly Karpov, representing the Soviet Union, and Viktor Korchnoi, who at that time was stateless. Korchnoi had defected from the Soviet Union two years earlier. Under such politically charged circumstances, there was always going to be enormous tension during the match.

△ *During the 1978 World Championship final, Viktor Korchnoi (right) alleged that Anatoly Karpov's team employed underhand tactics.*

CODED YOGHURTS

In the middle of the second game, Karpov was handed a yoghurt. Korchnoi's camp issued a formal protest after the game, claiming that the delivery could convey a coded message: 'A yoghurt after move 20 could signify "We instruct you to offer a draw". The possibilities are limitless.' After this, it was decreed that Karpov could only have a particular flavour of yoghurt and that it should be served at a specific time by a designated waiter.

MIND GAMES

A Russian parapsychologist, Dr Vladimir Zukhar, sat at the front of the audience staring directly at Korchnoi for the entire game. One of Korchnoi's delegation countered the possibility of undue mental interference by handing Dr Zukhar a copy of the anti-Soviet novel *The Gulag Archipelago*, then sat behind him for the rest of the game prodding him with a ball-point pen.

For the record, Karpov won the match.

THE RUSSIANS AND CHESS

Chess reached Russia in the 9th century from Persia. Until the 20th century, in common with other countries, chess was mainly a game for intellectuals and the wealthy. But after the October Revolution of 1917, chess gripped the Russian Empire's vast population as a result of an extraordinary and unique social experiment.

△ The Soviet Union was the world's first Communist country. It was founded in 1922, four years after the Bolsheviks, headed by Lenin, seized power.

△ Nikolai Krylenko initiated a major programme for the development of chess in the Soviet Union.

CHESS AND COMMUNISM

After the Communists came to power they were faced with the challenge of educating the people in the principles of Marxism, the political and economic theories on which the Soviet Union was based. By promoting chess, the government hoped to instil the rudiments of scientific, rational thinking in its people and weaken the grip of the Russian Orthodox Church, which was considered an enemy of Communism.

THE GREAT PLAN

Lenin, the first Communist leader, was a keen chess-player. After he died in 1924, Nikolai Krylenko, Commissar for War in the first Communist government, helped popularize chess. Soon there were chess clubs in factories and schools all over the country. When young players showed a particular talent they would be given special tuition. Krylenko's ambitious programme was a great success. By 1936, 700,000 players took part in the Soviet Trade Union championship. In the early 1970s, there were some four million registered chess players in the Soviet Union.

△ During the 1930s, chess clubs were formed across the Soviet Union – in factories, libraries, farms and in the army.

'RKERSI'

'EVERY CHESS-PLAYING WORKER IN THE USSR IS A LEADER OF SOCIALIST COMPETITION IN INDUSTRY.'

'CHESS IS A TRUE WEAPON AGAINST RELIGIOUS DELUSIONS.'

FIRST SUCCESS

From this mass movement it was inevitable that champions would be produced. The first great international success was Mikhail Botvinnik, who won the famous Nottingham tournament of 1936. In the main Soviet newspaper, *Pravda*, Botvinnik thanked Stalin, 'beloved teacher and leader', for inspiring his victory. In the Soviet Union, politics and chess went hand in hand. Botvinnik's success heralded the Soviet domination of world chess after World War II.

△ *Mikhail Botvinnik (left) became the first ever Soviet World Champion in 1948. He was hard-working, logical and totally loyal to the Communist cause.*

SOVIET SUPREMACY

From 1948 until 1972, every single World Champion was Soviet. Success bred more success. Botvinnik set up a chess school based on his scientific and methodical approach to the game from which many players benefited, including future World Champions Anatoly Karpov and Garry Kasparov.

THE FUTURE

With the collapse of the Communist regime in 1991, and with it the break up of the Soviet Union, state funding for chess virtually disappeared. However, with such a strong chess tradition, excellent players continue to come out of the region, and their dominance is likely to continue for many years to come.

◁ *Struggles on the board, such as the Fischer–Spassky World Championship match of 1972, mirrored the intense political rivalry, known as the Cold War, between the Soviet Union and the USA.*

COMPUTERS AND CHESS

Since the pioneering days of computer science in the 1940s, researchers have developed and constructed chess-playing machines. It was not until the late 1980s, however, that computers became powerful enough to take on the strongest players in the world.

◁ Early computer pioneers, such as Alan Turing, believed that constructing chess-playing programs would be of enormous benefit to their work.

◁ In 1769, the Hungarian inventor Baron Wolfgang Von Kemplen exhibited his chess-playing automaton, The Turk. *This mechanical figure appeared to move the pieces by itself. It was, in fact, operated by a person concealed inside the lower compartment.*

HOW DOES A COMPUTER PLAY CHESS?

The best human chess-players, using intuition, will examine perhaps just two or three moves in a position. After studying them each in turn, the player will decide which is the best.

A computer 'thinks' about chess in a very different way. First, it will examine all possible moves in a position and then all the possible moves after those moves, and so on. It doesn't take long before the computer has examined literally millions of different positions. Each position has a pre-programmed value, so the computer can calculate the best move.

While a computer examines far more positions, a human player is much more selective about the number of moves initially considered. Some people argue that humans, therefore, actually look into a position in much greater depth than a computer.

▽ The Phantom *is a chess computer with a difference. Using the latest technology, it is able to move its own pieces.*

Did you know ?

Chess is ideal for playing on the Internet. You can log onto the World Wide Web and find thousands of people all over the world playing chess. If you are interested in playing, turn to page 60 for a list of websites.

◁ *The latest chess computers can play at many different levels and often have famous games pre-programmed in their memory. These machines are an excellent way to improve your game.*

HOW TO BEAT YOUR CHESS COMPUTER

Chess-playing computers of a high standard are now available to everyone. They present a different kind of challenge to a human opponent. Here are some tips to help you beat your chess computer.

- Start on the lowest level, then build up.
- Computers are brilliant at short-term tactics, so take great care over your pieces. Watch out for tricks like forks and pins.
- Computers are less good at long-term planning – humans are much better in this respect. For example, if you see a potential weak point across the other side of the board, make sure that you exploit it.
- If all else fails, pull out the plug!

CHESS DATABASES

The computer's capacity to store huge amounts of information has revolutionized chess. Every professional player carries a lap-top computer containing millions of games from top-class events. With a couple of key-hits it's possible to recall the past games of opponents, then search for weaknesses in their play, just as any football manager will study the opposing team's defence on video before a match.

◁ *In 1999, Garry Kasparov took on a world team over the Internet. After four months and a tightly-fought contest, Kasparov finally won.*

'If a computer can beat the World Champion, a computer can read the best books in the world, can write the best plays, and can know everything about history and literature and people.'
Garry Kasparov, World Chess Champion

THE ULTIMATE CHALLENGE

In May 1997, a chess match took place that would make headlines all over the world. Garry Kasparov, the reigning World Chess Champion, and arguably the greatest player in the history of the game, sat down to face *Deep Blue*, a 1.4-tonne computer built and operated by a team of US scientists.

KASPAROV VERSUS *DEEP BLUE*

The *Deep Blue* team had tried twice before to defeat Garry Kasparov, in 1989 and 1996. On both occasions the computer had been crushed. In 1997, they met for another six-game match. The IBM team behind *Deep Blue* was confident that their machine was now good enough to defeat the World Champion. However, when Garry Kasparov was asked before the match whether the unthinkable might happen, he replied, 'I don't think it is an appropriate thing to discuss whether I might lose. I never lose. I have never lost in my life'.

◁ *One of* Deep Blue*'s massive processors. The name* Deep Blue *combines the orginal name of the project,* Deep Thought, *with IBM's nickname,* Big Blue.

△ *Sitting opposite Kasparov (right) is one of the* Deep Blue *team, ready to play the machine's moves as they appear on screen.*

THE BIG FIGHT

As the match progressed it became clear that *Deep Blue* was far stronger than in previous years. Going into the sixth and final game, the scores were level. And then for the first time in his career, Kasparov cracked up. After just one hour – an average game at the top level of chess lasts about four hours – his position lay in ruins. At the closing ceremony Kasparov was livid. He raged that if *Deep Blue* were to play in a regular tournament, he would 'tear it to pieces'.

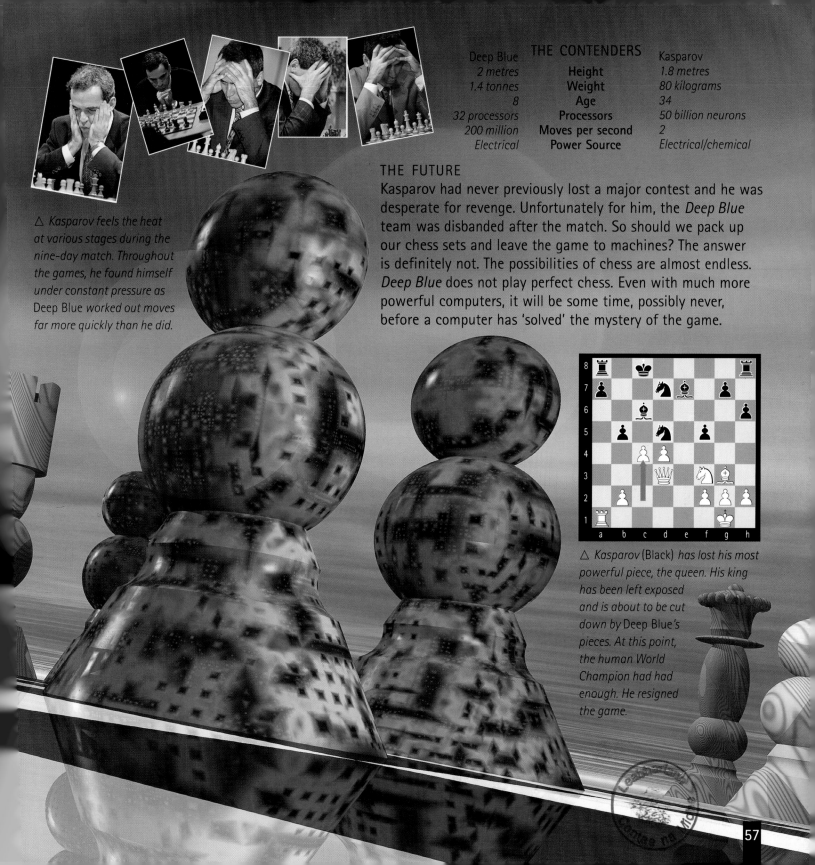

	THE CONTENDERS	
Deep Blue		Kasparov
2 metres	Height	1.8 metres
1.4 tonnes	Weight	80 kilograms
8	Age	34
32 processors	Processors	50 billion neurons
200 million	Moves per second	2
Electrical	Power Source	Electrical/chemical

△ Kasparov feels the heat at various stages during the nine-day match. Throughout the games, he found himself under constant pressure as Deep Blue worked out moves far more quickly than he did.

THE FUTURE

Kasparov had never previously lost a major contest and he was desperate for revenge. Unfortunately for him, the *Deep Blue* team was disbanded after the match. So should we pack up our chess sets and leave the game to machines? The answer is definitely not. The possibilities of chess are almost endless. *Deep Blue* does not play perfect chess. Even with much more powerful computers, it will be some time, possibly never, before a computer has 'solved' the mystery of the game.

△ Kasparov (Black) has lost his most powerful piece, the queen. His king has been left exposed and is about to be cut down by Deep Blue's pieces. At this point, the human World Champion had had enough. He resigned the game.

GLOSSARY

The following pages contain some of the more common terms used in chess. Not all of these terms are used in this book, but they may be useful if you read other books on the subject.

Blindfold chess A game in which the player cannot see the board – it isn't absolutely necessary to wear a blindfold! Players visualize the positions in their head and call out their moves using chess notation.

Check A piece that directly attacks the king is said to 'give check' or put it 'in check'. (*See pages 20–21*)

Checkmate The end of the game when the king is put in check and cannot escape. (*See pages 20–21*)

Combination A sequence of moves leading to material gain or checkmate.

Correspondence chess (or postal chess) A game of chess played by post. Moves are recorded in chess notation and sent to the opponent. Books may be consulted and analysis carried out on a board before deciding on a move.

Development Bringing pieces out at the start of the game. Having a 'lead in development' can be of crucial importance.

Diagonal A line of squares running obliquely across the board, along which the bishop is able to move, as well as the queen. Diagonals are identified by naming the squares at either end, for instance, the b1-h7 diagonal.

Discovered check When a piece moves, enabling a second piece to give check. (*See page 32–33*)

Double attack One piece attacks two pieces at the same time. A knight fork is an example of a double attack.

Double check Two pieces put the king in check at the same time. This occurs when a discovered check is played and both pieces give check.

Endgame or Ending The third phase of the game after the opening and the middlegame. In the endgame just a few pieces remain on the board. Strategy is quite different from the first two phases. For instance, as mating attacks are rare, the king becomes a powerful piece. Ultimately, the aim is to force a pawn to the eighth rank to get a new queen.

En prise A piece that is attacked but isn't defended is said to be 'en prise'. Likewise, a piece that is attacked by one less valuable than itself is also 'en prise', for example, when a knight attacks a queen. ('Prise' rhymes with 'cheese'.)

Exchange, an When pieces of equal value are swapped off the board. For instance, 'a bishop exchange' means that both sides have given up a bishop. (Note that this is different from 'the exchange', *see below*.)

Exchange, the This is a trade of particular pieces – a rook for a knight, or a rook for a bishop. If one player has lost a rook or a knight, for example, he or she is said to be 'the exchange down'.

Fianchetto The knight's pawn is advanced one square, creating room for the bishop to develop on the longest diagonal – on g2 or b2 if you are White, b7 or g7 if you are Black. Although at the side of the board, the bishop nevertheless exerts influence over the entire board.

FIDE (Fédération Internationale des Échecs) The world's governing body for chess, founded in 1924 in Paris. FIDE has many responsibilities. It determines the more obscure rules of the game, awards titles such as Master and Grandmaster, and hosts the chess Olympics.

File A line of eight squares running up the board. These vertical columns are often referred to by a letter, for instance, 'Black's rooks can enter the position down the c-file'.

Flank One side of the board.

Fork When two enemy pieces are attacked by a single piece, usually a knight. (*See pages 30–31*)

Gambit An opening in which material is given up to gain a lead in development. Usually this is a pawn or two, but sometimes a gambit can involve sacrificing a more important piece such as a knight or a bishop. (*See page 28*)

Grandmaster Apart from World Champion, the highest title in chess. Out of the millions of serious players in the world, there are just a few hundred who have been awarded the title 'Grandmaster' from FIDE. The full title is actually 'International Grandmaster', although this isn't used so frequently.

Initiative If you have the initiative you have more control over the game and can make threats to put your opponent on the defensive. Holding 'the initiative' gives you options, but it must be converted into something more tangible.

International Master The next title down from Grandmaster.

Isolated pawn A pawn is said to be isolated if there are no pawns of its own colour on adjacent files. In other words, it cannot be protected by another pawn so, in theory at least, it is more vulnerable to attack.

Kingside The half of the board on which the king stands at the beginning of the game. In other words, the right-hand side of the board from White's point of view. Even if the king moves away to the left, the kingside remains the half of the board where the king was standing at the beginning. (*See* Queenside)

Major piece A queen or a rook.

Material A term for pieces often used in a more general sense when discussing values. For example, 'White loses material', means that White loses more pieces than Black.

Middlegame The second of the three phases of the game. All pieces have been developed and the real battle has begun. (*See* Opening *and* Endgame)

Minor piece A knight or a bishop.

Open file A file on which there are no pawns, making it possible for a rook or a queen to penetrate deep into the enemy position. Sometimes controlling the only 'open file' is enough for a player to force a win.

Opening, an A planned system at the beginning of the game such as the Spanish Opening.

Opening, the The first phase of the game. Pieces are brought out and the king finds safety. (*See pages 28–29*)

Passed pawn A pawn that has no enemy pawn in front of it or on an adjacent file. Potentially, this gives the pawn a free run to the eighth rank where it can become a queen.

Pin A piece is attacked but cannot move because a piece behind it, usually of greater value, would then be taken. (*See page 31*)

Problem A composed position with a set number of moves to force a win or a draw.

Promotion When a pawn reaches the eighth rank it may turn into any other piece – knight, bishop, rook or queen. Because the queen is so powerful other pieces are rarely selected. (*See page 17*)

Queenside The half of the board on which the queen stands at the start of the game – from White's point of view, the left hand side of the board. Even if the queen moves to the other half of the board, the queenside remains the half of the board where the queen stood at the beginning of the game. (*See* Kingside)

Rank The rows of squares that run across the board, denoted by the numbers 1 to 8.

Resignation When a player knows that defeat is inevitable, he or she may give up the game before mate occurs.

Sacrifice When material is given up in order to gain an advantage, such as more pieces, in the long run. (*See pages 34–35*)

Score sheet The official document on which moves are recorded during a game. All tournament games must be recorded – it is part of the official rules of chess.

Simultaneous exhibition An event in which a Grandmaster or expert takes on a number of weaker players at once. Usually up to 30 players are taken on, but the record is reputedly held by a Yugoslav chess journalist, Dmitri Bjelica, who played 301 players simultaneously in 1982. The display lasted 9 hours – he won 258, drew 36 and lost 7.

Skewer When two pieces are attacked along the same line. Usually, it is the most valuable piece that is attacked first. After this piece has moved, the piece of lesser value behind it is captured.

Stalemate When the player whose turn it is cannot make any legal moves but is not in check. The game ends as a draw. (*See page 39*)

Strategy Long-term planning.

Tactics This has a distinct meaning in chess. A tactic is a short-term operation, usually played to win material. The more common tactics have acquired colourful names such as 'skewer'.

Tempo, tempi A unit of time expressed in terms of a move. For instance, if the queen advances, but then has to retreat on the next turn, it could be said that a tempo has been lost (one move). If several tempi have been lost, then several moves have been wasted.

Time trouble All serious tournament games are played within a time limit, using a special chess clock. The standard time limit for tournament games is 40 moves in 2 hours for each player, followed by another 20 moves in 1 hour if the game is unfinished. When players mishandle their time allocation and must make several moves quickly to reach the required number of moves, they are said to be 'in time trouble' or 'under time pressure'. Some players are time pressure addicts, who seem able to move only with the rush of adrenalin that comes when the clock approaches zero hour.

Under-promotion When a pawn reaches the eighth rank, but a piece other than the queen is selected.

Zugzwang A German word meaning 'compulsion to move'. Occasionally a situation occurs in which any move a player makes will compromise his or her position. It would be better to 'pass', but this is not possible.

ANSWERS AND RESOURCES

ANSWERS TO PAGES 12–16

Page 12: The king can take either the knight on d6, the pawn on d7, or the rook on f8.

Page 13: The rook can capture either the pawn on d6, or the knight on c1.

Page 14: The bishop is only able to capture one piece: the pawn on a2.

Page 15: The queen can capture either the rook on e7, the knight on b6, or the pawn on f2.

Page 16: The knight can capture either the pawn on e3, the bishop on b4, or the rook on c7.

TEST POSITIONS, PAGES 40-41

1 *Black should promote to a queen with 1 ...e1(Q) – which actually puts White in checkmate.*

2 *By far the best move is to play 1 ...Nxg3, winning a bishop at no cost. It is illegal for White to capture the knight with the pawn – this would put the king in check from the bishop on b6.*

CONTACT ADDRESSES

British Chess Federation
The Watch Oak,
Chain Lane,
Battle,
East Sussex TN33 OYD,
England
tel: +44 (0) 1424-775222
e: office@bcf.org.uk
www.bcf.org.uk

Chess Scotland
15 Hope Street,
Glasgow,
Scotland
tel: +44 (0) 141-221-6464
e: office@chessscotland.com
www.chessscotland.com

Welsh Chess Union
Executive Director: Mark Adams,
8 Museum Court,
Griffithstown,
Torfaen NP4 5GZ,
Wales
tel: +44 (0) 1495-758299
www.welshchessunion.co.uk

Irish Chess Union
17 The Hardwicke,
Brunswick Street,
Dublin 7,
Republic of Ireland
tel: +44 (0) 3531-8782436
e: shannon@iol.ie
www.irishchessunion.com

THE INTERNET

There are many websites dedicated to playing chess:

The Internet Chess Club (ICC), **www.chessclub.com**, *is open to players of all abilities. Some of the top players in the world gather here. There is a subscription charge.*

www.playchess.com *is a rapidly growing playing site. There are online lectures, computer chess areas, and also special beginners' rooms. There is a subscription charge for full access to the site.*

The US-based World Chess Network is a comprehensive site. You can play online, shop at an online store, and get tuition from top players. Free. **www.worldchessnetwork.com**

MSN has a less high-powered site at: **www.zone.com**. *Free.*

You can play chess and other classic board games on **yahoo.com** – *just head for the Games section. It is user-friendly and has a ranking system. Free.*

3 *The best way to meet the threat from White is to move the king away from the middle as quickly as possible by castling: 1 ...0–0. Tucked behind the pawns, Black's king is quite safe.*

4 *White should capture the pawn in the middle with the bishop: 1 Bxd5, exploiting the pin. If the bishop is captured 1 ...Bxd5, then White takes the rook with 2 Rxa7. If it isn't captured, then White will take the bishop on b7. In either case, White has a winning material advantage.*

5 *White can play 1 Rh3+, skewering king and rook. Black's king must move, for instance: 1 ...Kf2. White can then capture the rook on the other side of the board: 2 Rxa3.*

6 *Black can checkmate in one move: 1 ...Qh2 mate.*

7 *White has a lethal discovered check: 1 Rf2+. Black's king must move out of the check from the bishop: 1 ...Kg8, then White takes the queen, 2 Rxg2, giving a decisive material advantage.*

8 *There is more than one good move here, but the best is to sacrifice the queen with 1 Qxc5+. If Black plays 1 ...Qxc5, then White delivers a crushing blow with 2 Bxa6 checkmate.*

9 *White has a very sneaky way to win from this position. White plays 1 g8(Q)+. Black, of course, must capture the new queen: 1 ...Kxg8, but then comes a knight fork: 2 Ne7+. After Black's king moves out of check, the knight takes the rook. With an extra knight, White should be able to win the game.*

10 *White can still draw the game with this amazing defence: 1 Qg8+. Black must capture the queen, 1 ...Kxg8, but then White has no legal move. As White is not in check, then the position is stalemate – a draw.*

INDEX

ACKNOWLEDGEMENTS

The publishers would like to thank the following illustrators for their contribution to this book: **Julie Hartigan** 42-43, 48-49, 54-55; all other illustrations created by **Mike Buckley**.

The publishers would like to thank the following for supplying photographs:

6 l AKG London/British Museum, London; tc The Art Archive; bc AKG London/British Museum, London; 7 tc The Bridgeman Art Library/British Library, London; r AKG London/British Museum, London; bl The Bridgeman Art Library/Musée Conde, Chantilly, France; 8 tl The Art Archive/Bibliothèque Nationale Paris; cl AKG London/Erich Lessing; bl Christies Images; b Christies Images; 8-9 bl Christies Images; 9 tr Mary Evans Picture Library; cr The Kobal Collection; br Mattel Interactive; 42 tl Mary Evans Picture Library; tc (Capablanca) Hulton Getty; tc (Alekhine) Hulton Getty; tcr (Euwe) Hulton Getty; tcr (Lasker) Hulton Getty; tr (Botvinnik) Society for Cooperation in Russian and Soviet Studies (SCR) Photo Library Photo Library/Novosti; 43 t (Petrosian) SCR Photo Library/Novosti; tl (Smyslov) Topham Picture Point; tc (Fischer) Topham Picture Point; tcl (Tal) SCR/Novosti; tc (Spassky) SCR Photo Library/Novosti; tcr (Karpov) Topham Picture Point; tr (Kasparov) SCR Photo Library/Novosti; 45 tr Sovfoto; CR Rex Features/Jorgensen; bl Topham Picture Point; 46 tl SCR Photo Library/Novosti; tc SCR Photo Library/Novosti; bc Topham Picture Point/Associated Press; 46-47 t IBM; 47 c Allsport UK Ltd/Chris Cole; 49 tc SCR Photo Library/Novosti; 50 c SCR Photo Library/Novosti; 50-51 repeat image in digital a/w SCR Photo Library/Novosti; 51 tl Hulton Getty; 52 tl SCR Photo Library; cl Hulton Getty; bl SCR Photo Library; 53 tr SCR Photo Library; bl Frank Spooner Pictures/D.

Kennerly-Liaison; bc Hulton Getty; 54 tr Science Photo Library; cl AKG London; 55 tl Frank Spooner Pictures/Barr-Liaison; bc www.zone.com/kasparov; 56 c Rex Features; bl Popperfoto/Jeff Christensen/Reuters; 57 tl (*Deep Blue*) Frank Spooner Pictures/Swanson/Liaison; tl Rex Features/Andre Camara; tc Rex Features/Erik Pendzich; tr (*Deep Blue*) Popperfoto/Peter Morgan/Reuters; tr Rex Features/Erik Pendzich.

Key: b = bottom, c = centre, l=left, t = top, r = right.

Every effort has been made to trace the copyright holders of the photographs. The publishers apologize for any omissions.

The author would like to thank Bob Kendall, Nigel Povah and especially Mairéad and Declan.